Twice
the love

A Workbook for Kids in Blended Families

If you're reading this book, it means your family is getting bigger. You probably live with Mom or Dad, and your parent is ready to welcome new people into his or her life. Maybe a new grownup is joining your family, or you're getting new brothers or sisters. Or maybe you're moving into a house with another group of people. It must be scary. You may feel like things are changing, and you don't like it. It'll take a while, but soon you'll find that a blended family gives you twice the love!

Draw a picture in the box below of you and your mom or dad.
You can also add brothers, sisters, grandparents, or pets.

Memories

A family can have many good memories. These memories can come from special occasions like vacations, holidays, or other celebrations. Good memories can also come from everyday activities like bedtime stories, watching a movie, or playing together. But sometimes memories aren't so good—families can have sad times too. All families are like this.

Draw or write about one good memory you have of your family.

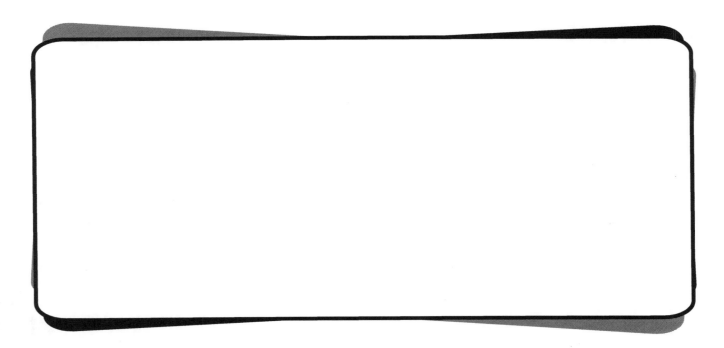

Draw or write about one bad memory you have of your family.

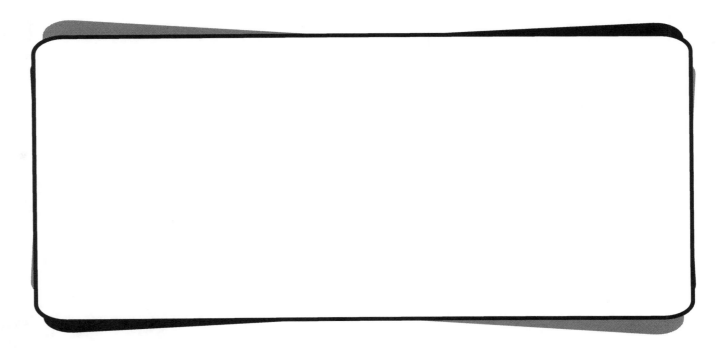

It Can't Be True!

When your mom or dad told you your family would be blending, you may have been unhappy because you liked things the way they were. You may not want your mom or dad to have a new grownup friend, or you may not want to share your mom or dad with new brothers and sisters. You may tell yourself it just can't be happening, or pretend it isn't. Pretend you're going on a journey to a place that makes you happy. Draw or write about four things that happen on your journey there.

It's All My Fault

Children sometimes blame themselves if their mom or dad is unhappy. If one of your parents is upset about your new blended family, you may feel like it's your fault your family is changing. It's not your fault. As you grow older, you can choose more things about your life. There are some things, though, that a child can't choose. Color the stars that show things a child can choose.

Friends

Favorite Food

Parents

Where to Live

Favorite Toy

Bedtime

Draw a picture of your blended family in the box below. How has your family changed?

Stepmom

My stepmom brought her stuff today

It really made me mad

She moved right in and changed the house

She even changed my dad

She makes my bacon way too crisp

She tries to fix my hair

But when she shops for nail polish

She buys enough to share

To make it worse, she brought her cat

It hides beneath my bed

And then she made me go with her

To a hill where we could sled

My stepmom isn't like me

And there are different rules

But just between the two of us

My stepmom's kinda cool

The little girl in this poem isn't sure how she feels about her stepmother moving in. Describe how you feel about your new parent.

When families blend, things can become confusing. People must learn to share spaces. Rules sometimes change. Schedules change. It can be upsetting if you don't understand these changes. Color the things that will help you understand and get along with others.

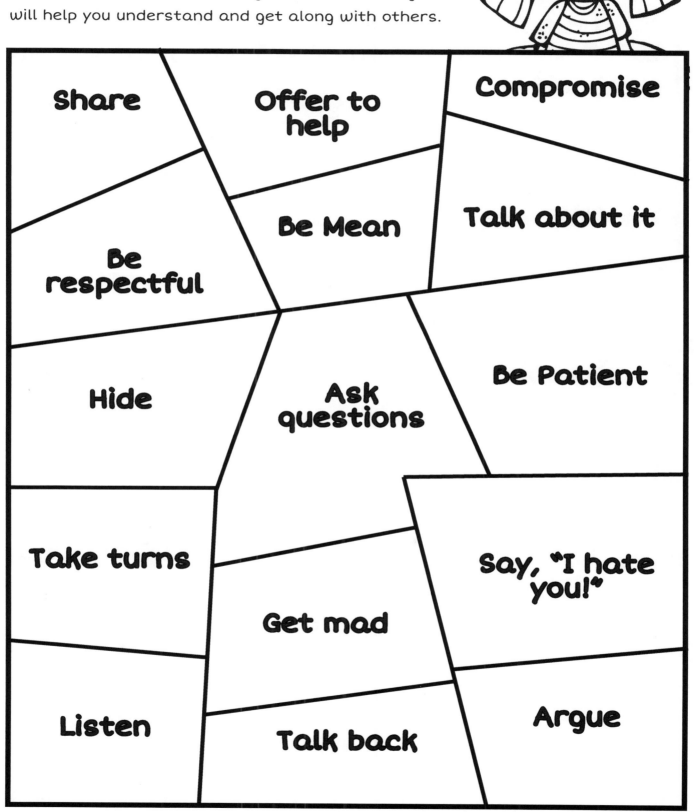

Share

Offer to help

Compromise

Be Mean

Talk about it

Be respectful

Hide

Ask questions

Be Patient

Take turns

Say, "I hate you!"

Get mad

Listen

Talk back

Argue

Simon Says
A blended family often means new rules. It can be hard to remember how rules change.

Old Rules	New Rules
Make bed	Do homework
Do homework	Take bath before bed
Be respectful	Fold clothes
Do dishes	Make bed
Walk dog	Be respectful

What are some old rules at your house?

What are some new rules at your house?

Bringing two families together requires a lot of cooperation.
Draw a picture of your family working together.

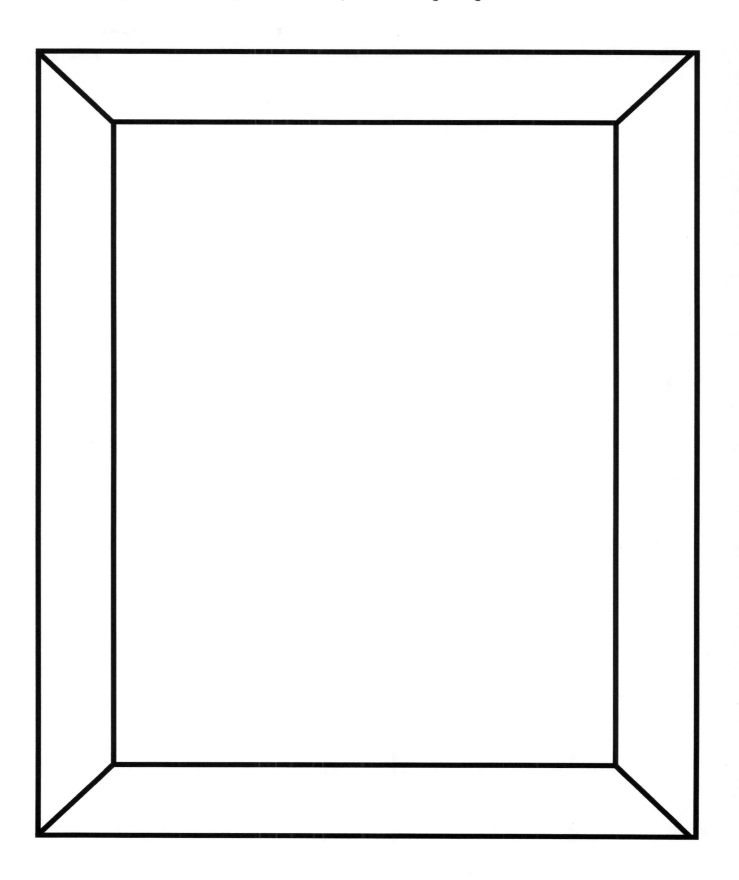

Favorites Some family members will like the same things, while some will like different things. Ask each member of your blended family about their favorite things below, and write their choices in the circles.

Ice Cream

Color

Holiday

Animal

Draw

When two families come together, it may feel like no one is listening. Use the space below to write a letter to your mom or dad about what's important to you.

Worries

Blending two families can make you worry. That is normal. Everyone worries—even your mom or dad. Color the things that make you worry.

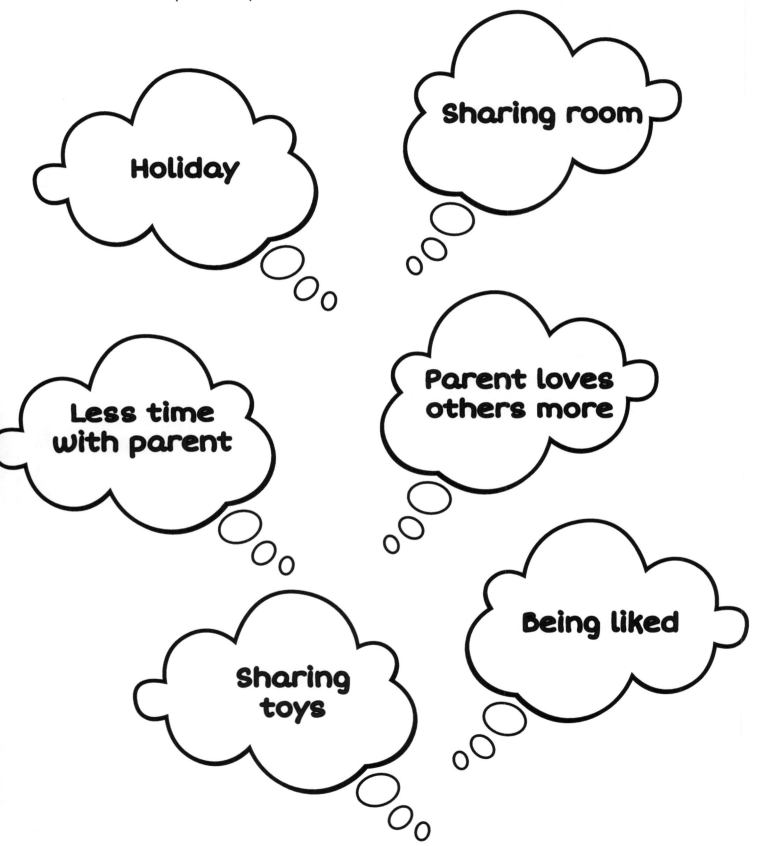

Families come in all shapes and sizes. Some families are big, some are small. Families can also come in different colors, and believe in different things. Below, draw or paste three pictures of different kinds of families.

Everyone has to follow rules—moms follow rules, dads follow rules. You have rules to follow, too. Remember: When families come together, rules often change. People may have different rules because they're old or younger, and because they have different responsiblities. Pretend you're the mom or dad and want to keep you children safe. What rules would you create for a small child and big child?

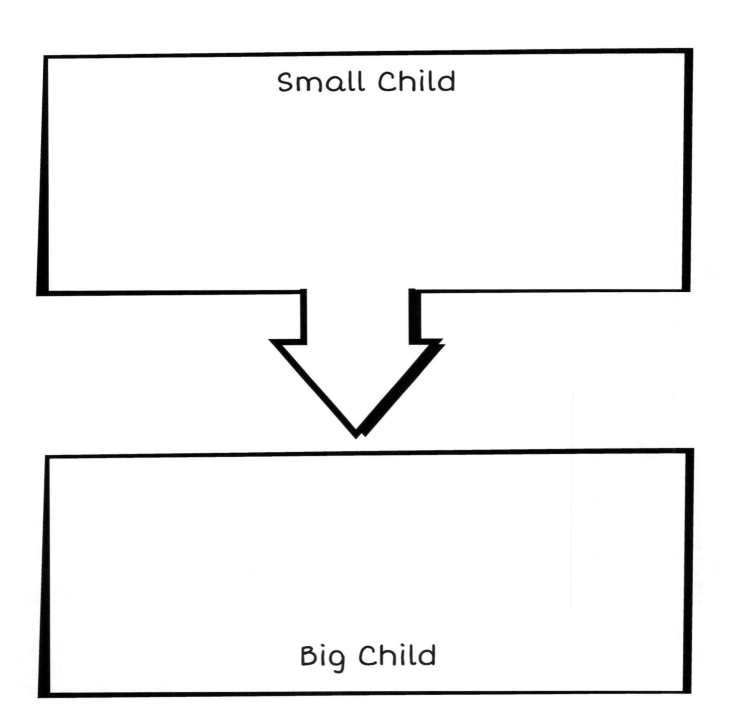

Small Child

Big Child

No two people are the same. Even twins like different things and behave in different ways. You're different from your mom and dad and other members of your family. Being different is not bad—the things that make you different make you special and unique.

Blending families will change things. You may feel sad about things you miss. In the box below, write or draw a picture about things you miss now that your family has gotten bigger.

Blended families can be a lot of fun too! Everyone brings different talents and interests to a family. In the box below, draw a picture of your blended family doing something you've never done before.

Blended families may celebrate differently, which isn't a bad thing!

Think of a holiday your family celebrates. Make a plan with your family about how you'll celebrate the holiday this year.

Name of holiday: _____

Are you going somewhere, or are people coming to meet you?

What foods will you eat?

How will you celebrate?

How will this celebration be the same as it was before?

How will it be different, now that you have a blended family?

Now that your family is bigger, you'll have new adventures. Adventures are fun! Talk with your family, and plan an adventure to go on together. It may be a visit to a park, a car trip, building something together, or something completely different!

Name of adventure: _____

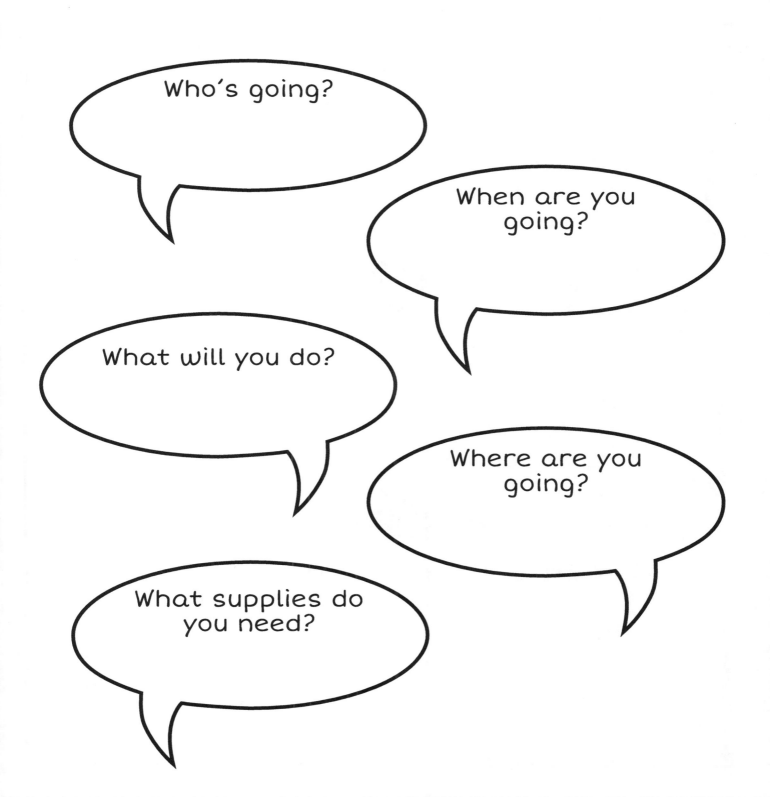

Blending families means compromising and discovering new things. In the top and bottom boxes below, list things you and your new family members each like to do. In the middle, list things you both like to do. Now, color the top box blue, the middle box green, and the bottom box yellow. Blue plus yellow makes green!

Things you like to do

Things both you and your new family members like to do

Things your new family members like to do

Jealousy means wanting something someone else has. It can make you very unhappy. You could be jealous of many things, like how much time someone spends with someone else, toys or other things someone has, or even what other people get to do. You may even feel like your parent loves someone else more than you. Jealousy can make you feel angry, sad, or rejected. You can't control feeling jealous, but you can control how you react to it.

Below, draw an X through the things people do when they get jealous.

Draw a picture of a jealous person in the box below.

Why is this person jealous?

What are some good ways to get over his or her jealousy?

Families share many things. You may have to share your bedroom, toys, bathroom, or even time with your mom or dad. It can be hard to share.

Name three things your mom or dad shares with you.

1. _____

2. _____

3. _____

Name three things a friend shares with you.

1. _____

2. _____

3. _____

Name three things you can share with others.

1. _____

2. _____

3. _____

It's important to get to know your new family members. Ask each new family member these questions:

What do you like to do in the summer?

What is something you don't like to do?

What's your favorite thing to do?

What's something you'd like to learn how to do?

Did you find anything that you and your new family members have in common? If so, what?

Draw a picture of you and your new family members doing something fun together.

Describe what you're doing:

_____

_____

Would You Rather?

Ask a new family member the questions below, and circle his or her responses.

Would you rather...

- be banned from a computer forever?   OR   not be allowed to eat anything sweet forever?

- be able to control the weather?   OR   be able to talk to animals?

- have bright-green teeth?   OR   have bright-green hair?

- be able to fly?   OR   be able to turn invisible?

- have one eye in the middle of your head like Cyclops?   OR   have two noses?

- eat only your favorite food forever?   OR   only eat your favorite food one more time ever?

- have seven arms?   OR   have seven legs?

Everyone is unique. Just like a snowflake, there is no one just like you. Fill in the heart below with words or pictures that describe you.

You and your new family members will have many special times together. In the hexagon shape below, draw a picture of something special you want to do with your family.

Respect is important. It means being considerate of other people and their things. You should be respectful to others, and expect others to show respect to you too.

It is also important to have self-respect. Self-respect means caring about yourself. To have self-respect, you should always try your best, and try not to do things you know are wrong. Draw an X through the statements below that are disrespectful.

How can you show others respect?

_____

_____

Calling people bad names is very disrespectful. Make a poster below by cutting out or drawing pictures that show people being respectful to each other.

Sometimes, it's hard to agree with others!

Pretend you and a friend both want to do different things today: You want to go to the park, and he or she wants to go to a movie. How can you compromise you both get what you want? Write or draw it below.

Pretend you and your parent want you to do different things today: You want to play with a friend, but your mom or dad wants you to clean your room. How do you respectfully tell your parent you want to play with your friend? Can you suggest a compromise? Write or draw it below.

It's important that all your family members work together as a team. Working together as a team means that everyone listens to each other and does their part to get something done. Ask your family members to help you write a story by filling in the blanks below.

1. Family member's name: _____

2. An animal: _____

3. A place: _____

4. A game: _____

5. Another family member's name: _____

6. A yucky vegetable: _____

7. A place: _____

8. A pet's name: _____

9. Another animal: _____

10. A thing: _____

1. _____ wanted to take his/her 2. _____ to the

3. _____ to play 4. _____, but he/she couldn't because

5. _____ needed some 6. _____ from the 7. _____.

1. _____ wanted to help 5. _____, so he/she put

8. _____ on a leash and walked to the 7. _____ to buy

6. _____. On the way there, 8. _____ saw a(n)

9. _____ and chased it up a 10. _____.

1. _____ climbed the 10. _____ and rescued the

9. _____. 5. _____ was very thankful that

1. _____ was so kind, so he/she gave him/her a big kiss!

You and your family want to build a treehouse together. Draw a picture of everyone working together to build the treehouse.

You and your family want to build a treehouse together. Draw a picture of everyone working together to build the treehouse.

Your Goal
_____

Family Member 1's Goal
_____

Family Member 2's Goal
_____

Family Member 3's Goal
_____

Family Member 4's Goal
_____

Family Member 5's Goal
_____

Family Member 6's Goal
_____

Families are a lot of fun and a lot of frustration. Every family goes through unhappy times. It's important to talk about things that bother you, and to listen to what others have to say. It's also very important to always be polite and respectful. Your new family members care about you and want you to like them as much as you want them to like you. Remember: Blended families mean twice the love! In the scroll below, write a letter to your new family members, welcoming them to your family.

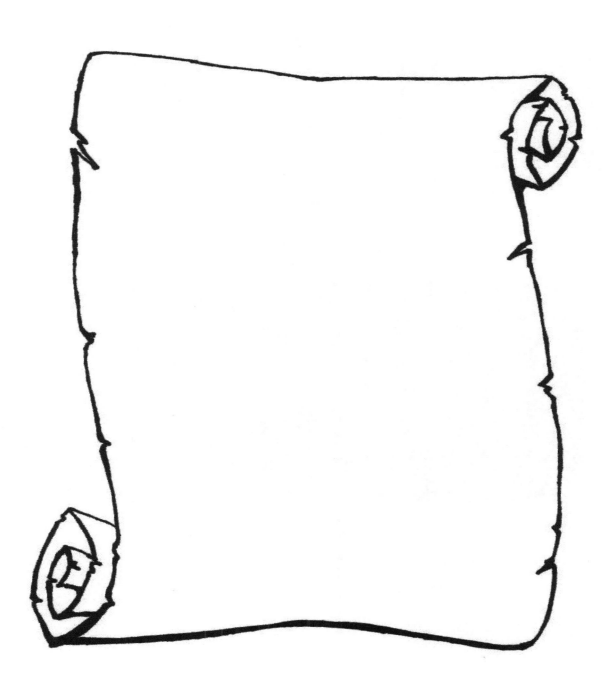

Now that you've completed this workbook, keep it to help you when you feel angry, sad, or lonely because of the changes in your life. Remember that your new family members are going through the same kinds of changes and feelings. You can help them feel better, too!

HOW TO USE THIS REFLECTION JOURNAL

Now that you've completed the activities in this workbook, it's time to focus on putting everything you learned into practice.

What does that mean? It means using the things you've learned to help you each day.

Make a plan for each morning; then at the end of the day, before bedtime, think about your day.

What was good about it?
What brought you joy?
What went wrong?
How did you handle it?
What can you do to have a great day tomorrow?

HOW TO USE THIS REFLECTION JOURNAL

STEP 1: Each morning make a plan for your day by completing Side 1 of that day's journal page.

STEP 2: Each evening complete side 2 as you reflect on your day.

DATE: S M T W TH F S ___ / ___ / ___

ONLY POSITIVE THOUGHTS IN MY DAY
I can make today awesome by:

_____

_____

_____

DRAW IT!

what are you
looking forward
to most today?

I LOVE MYSELF
LIST 3 THINGS YOU LOVE ABOUT YOURSELF

WHAT IS SOMETHING THAT MAKES YOU HAPPY

_____

_____

_____

TODAY I FELT

SOMETHING GREAT THAT HAPPENED TODAY

_____

_____

_____

 THIS PERSON BROUGHT ME JOY TODAY

_____

_____

DATE: S M T W TH F S ___/___/___

ONLY POSITIVE THOUGHTS IN MY DAY
I can make today awesome by:

_____

_____

_____

DRAW IT!
what are you looking forward to most today?

I LOVE MYSELF
list 3 words that describe you

WHAT DO YOU LIKE TO DO FOR FUN

_____

_____

_____

TODAY I FELT

SOMETHING GREAT THAT HAPPENED TODAY

_____

_____

_____

 THIS PERSON BROUGHT ME JOY TODAY

_____

_____

DATE: S M T W TH F S ___/___/___

ONLY POSITIVE THOUGHTS IN MY DAY
I can make today awesome by:

_____

_____

_____

DRAW IT!
what are you looking forward to most today?

I LOVE MYSELF
LIST 3 THINGS you are really good at doing

WHAT IS ONE OF YOUR FAVORITE MEMORIES

_____

_____

_____

TODAY I FELT

SOMETHING GREAT THAT HAPPENED TODAY

_____

_____

_____

 THIS PERSON BROUGHT ME JOY TODAY

_____

_____

DATE: S M T W TH F S ___/___/___

ONLY POSITIVE THOUGHTS IN MY DAY
I can make today awesome by:

_____

_____

_____

DRAW IT!

what are you
looking forward
to most today?

I LOVE MYSELF
LIST 3 THINGS YOU LOVE DOING

WHO IS A PERSON YOU ADMIRE (LIKE)

_____

_____

_____

TODAY I FELT

SOMETHING GREAT THAT HAPPENED TODAY

_____

_____

_____

 ## THIS PERSON BROUGHT ME JOY TODAY

_____

_____

DATE: S M T W TH F S ___/___/___

ONLY POSITIVE THOUGHTS IN MY DAY
I can make today awesome by:

_____

_____

_____

DRAW IT!
what are you looking forward to most today?

I LOVE MYSELF
LIST 3 THINGS YOU'D LIKE TO improve about yourself

WHAT IS SOMETHING THAT MAKES YOU PROUD?

_____

_____

_____

TODAY I FELT

SOMETHING GREAT THAT HAPPENED TODAY

_____

_____

_____

 THIS PERSON BROUGHT ME JOY TODAY

_____

_____

DATE: S M T W TH F S ___/___/___

ONLY POSITIVE THOUGHTS IN MY DAY

I can make today awesome by:

_____

_____

_____

DRAW IT!

what are you looking forward to most today?

I LOVE MYSELF

LIST 3 THINGS THAT BRING YOU HAPPINESS

WHO IS THE KINDEST PERSON YOU KNOW

_____

_____

_____

TODAY I FELT

SOMETHING GREAT THAT HAPPENED TODAY

_____

_____

_____

 THIS PERSON BROUGHT ME JOY TODAY

_____

_____

DATE: S M T W TH F S ___/___/___

ONLY POSITIVE THOUGHTS IN MY DAY
I can make today awesome by:

_____

_____

_____

DRAW IT!
what are you looking forward to most today?

I LOVE MYSELF
WRITE 3 WORDS TO DESCRIBE YOUR LIFE

DID I TRY SOMETHING NEW TODAY?

_____

_____

_____

TODAY I FELT

SOMETHING GREAT THAT HAPPENED TODAY

_____

_____

_____

 ## THIS PERSON BROUGHT ME JOY TODAY

_____

_____

DATE: S M T W TH F S ___/___/___

ONLY POSITIVE THOUGHTS IN MY DAY
I can make today awesome by:

_____

_____

_____

DRAW IT!

what are you looking forward to most today?

I LOVE MYSELF
LIST 3 THINGS WORDS TO DESCRIBE YOUR FAMILY

DID I GET OUT OF MY COMFORT ZONE TODAY?

_____

_____

_____

TODAY I FELT

SOMETHING GREAT THAT HAPPENED TODAY

_____

_____

_____

 ## THIS PERSON BROUGHT ME JOY TODAY

_____

_____

DATE: **S M T W TH F S** ___/___/___

💬 **ONLY POSITIVE THOUGHTS IN MY DAY**
I can make today awesome by:

_____

_____

_____

DRAW IT!

what are you looking forward to most today?

I LOVE MYSELF
LIST 3 THINGS YOU LOVE ABOUT YOURSELF

THIS IS WHAT I COULD HAVE DONE BETTER TODAY

_____

_____

_____

TODAY I FELT

SOMETHING GREAT THAT HAPPENED TODAY

_____

_____

_____

 THIS PERSON BROUGHT ME JOY TODAY

_____

_____

DATE: S M T W TH F S ___/___/___

ONLY POSITIVE THOUGHTS IN MY DAY

I can make today awesome by:

_____

_____

_____

DRAW IT!

what are you looking forward to most today?

I LOVE MYSELF

LIST 3 THINGS THAT MAKE YOU SMILE

TODAY I LEARNED THIS ABOUT MYSELF

_____

_____

_____

TODAY I FELT

SOMETHING GREAT THAT HAPPENED TODAY

_____

_____

_____

THIS PERSON BROUGHT ME JOY TODAY

_____

_____

DATE: S M T W TH F S ___/___/___

ONLY POSITIVE THOUGHTS IN MY DAY
I can make today awesome by:

_____

_____

_____

DRAW IT!

what are you looking forward to most today?

I LOVE MYSELF
WRITE 3 THINGS THAT ARE GREAT ABOUT YOU

WHAT I'M LOVING ABOUT LIFE RIGHT NOW

_____

_____

_____

TODAY I FELT

SOMETHING GREAT THAT HAPPENED TODAY

_____

_____

_____

 THIS PERSON BROUGHT ME JOY TODAY

_____

_____

DATE: S M T W TH F S ___/___/___

ONLY POSITIVE THOUGHTS IN MY DAY
I can make today awesome by:

_____

_____

_____

DRAW IT!

what are you looking forward to most today?

I LOVE MYSELF
NAME 3 PEOPLE WHO BRING YOU HAPPINESS

I HOPE TOMORROW LOOKS LIKE THIS

_____

_____

_____

TODAY I FELT

SOMETHING GREAT THAT HAPPENED TODAY

_____

_____

_____

 THIS PERSON BROUGHT ME JOY TODAY

_____

_____

DATE: S M T W TH F S ___/___/___

ONLY POSITIVE THOUGHTS IN MY DAY
I can make today awesome by:

_____

_____

_____

DRAW IT!

what are you
looking forward
to most today?

I LOVE MYSELF
NAME 3 THINGS YOUR FRIENDS THINK YOU ARE AWESOME AT

TOMORROW I WILL SHOW KINDNESS TO THIS PERSON

_____

_____

_____

TODAY I FELT

SOMETHING GREAT THAT HAPPENED TODAY

_____

_____

_____

 ## THIS PERSON BROUGHT ME JOY TODAY

_____

_____

DATE: S M T W TH F S ___/___/___

ONLY POSITIVE THOUGHTS IN MY DAY
I can make today awesome by:

_____

_____

_____

DRAW IT!

what are you looking forward to most today?

I LOVE MYSELF
WRITE 3 THINGS YOUR CLASSMATES SAY YOU ARE GREAT AT

THIS IS WHAT I WANT TO IMPROVE ABOUT MYSELF

_____

_____

_____

TODAY I FELT

SOMETHING GREAT THAT HAPPENED TODAY

_____

_____

_____

 THIS PERSON BROUGHT ME JOY TODAY

_____

_____

DATE: S M T W TH F S ___/___/___

ONLY POSITIVE THOUGHTS IN MY DAY

I can make today awesome by:

_____

_____

_____

DRAW IT!

what are you looking forward to most today?

I LOVE MYSELF

LIST 3 THINGS YOU DO THAT MAKES YOUR FAMILY HAPPY

TODAY I.....

_____

_____

_____

TODAY I FELT

😊 🙂 😐 🙁 😣 😴

SOMETHING GREAT THAT HAPPENED TODAY

_____

_____

_____

THIS PERSON BROUGHT ME JOY TODAY

_____

_____

DATE: S M T W TH F S ___/___/___

ONLY POSITIVE THOUGHTS IN MY DAY
I can make today awesome by:

_____
_____
_____

DRAW IT!

what are you looking forward to most today?

I LOVE MYSELF
LIST 3 THINGS THAT MAKE YOU HAPPY

WHAT I'M LOVING ABOUT LIFE RIGHT NOW

_____

_____

_____

TODAY I FELT

SOMETHING GREAT THAT HAPPENED TODAY

_____

_____

_____

 THIS PERSON BROUGHT ME JOY TODAY

_____

_____

DATE: S M T W TH F S ___/___/___

ONLY POSITIVE THOUGHTS IN MY DAY
I can make today awesome by:

_____

_____

_____

DRAW IT!

what are you looking forward to most today?

I LOVE MYSELF
LIST 3 THINGS THAT MAKE YOU FEEL GOOD

TODAY I WANT TO.....

_____

_____

_____

TODAY I FELT

SOMETHING GREAT THAT HAPPENED TODAY

_____

_____

_____

THIS PERSON BROUGHT ME JOY TODAY

_____

_____

DATE: S M T W TH F S _____/_____/_____

ONLY POSITIVE THOUGHTS IN MY DAY

I can make today awesome by:

_____

_____

_____

DRAW IT!

what are you looking forward to most today?

I LOVE MYSELF

LIST 3 FUTURE GOALS FOR YOURSELF

TODAY'S ACTIVITIES MADE ME.....

_____

_____

_____

TODAY I FELT

SOMETHING GREAT THAT HAPPENED TODAY

_____

_____

_____

 ## THIS PERSON BROUGHT ME JOY TODAY

_____

_____

DATE: S M T W TH F S ___/___/___

ONLY POSITIVE THOUGHTS IN MY DAY
I can make today awesome by:

_____

_____

_____

DRAW IT!
what are you looking forward to most today?

I LOVE MYSELF
LIST 3 THINGS YOU ENJOY DOING

TODAY I WANTED TO....

_____

_____

_____

TODAY I FELT

😊 🙂 😐 🙁 😣 😴

SOMETHING GREAT THAT HAPPENED TODAY

_____

_____

_____

☀ THIS PERSON BROUGHT ME JOY TODAY ☀

_____

_____

DATE: S M T W TH F S ___/___/___

ONLY POSITIVE THOUGHTS IN MY DAY
I can make today awesome by:

_____

_____

_____

DRAW IT!

what are you looking forward to most today?

I LOVE MYSELF
LIST 3 THINGS YOU DO THAT MAKES OTHERS SMILE

IF I COULD CHANGE THIS ABOUT TODAY

_____

_____

_____

TODAY I FELT

SOMETHING GREAT THAT HAPPENED TODAY

_____

_____

_____

THIS PERSON BROUGHT ME JOY TODAY

_____

_____

DATE: S M T W TH F S ___/___/___

ONLY POSITIVE THOUGHTS IN MY DAY
I can make today awesome by:

_____

_____

_____

DRAW IT!
what are you looking forward to most today?

I LOVE MYSELF
LIST 3 THINGS YOU LOVE ABOUT YOURSELF

MY DAY WAS.....

_____

_____

_____

TODAY I FELT

😊 😊 😐 ☹️ 😣 😴

SOMETHING GREAT THAT HAPPENED TODAY

_____

_____

_____

THIS PERSON BROUGHT ME JOY TODAY

_____

_____

DATE: S M T W TH F S ___/___/___

ONLY POSITIVE THOUGHTS IN MY DAY
I can make today awesome by:

_____

_____

_____

DRAW IT!

what are you looking forward to most today?

I LOVE MYSELF
WRITE 3 AFFIRMATIONS: I AM.....

I LEARNED THIS ABOUT MYSELF TODAY

_____

_____

_____

TODAY I FELT

SOMETHING GREAT THAT HAPPENED TODAY

_____

_____

_____

 THIS PERSON BROUGHT ME JOY TODAY

_____

_____

DATE: S M T W TH F S ___/___/___

ONLY POSITIVE THOUGHTS IN MY DAY

I can make today awesome by:

_____

_____

_____

DRAW IT!

what are you looking forward to most today?

I LOVE MYSELF

LIST 3 GOALS YOU'D LIKE TO ACHIEVE THIS WEEK

I HOPE TOMORROW IS....

_____

_____

_____

TODAY I FELT

SOMETHING GREAT THAT HAPPENED TODAY

_____

_____

_____

THIS PERSON BROUGHT ME JOY TODAY

_____

_____

DATE: S M T W TH F S ___/___/___

ONLY POSITIVE THOUGHTS IN MY DAY

I can make today awesome by:

_____

_____

_____

DRAW IT!

what are you looking forward to most today?

I LOVE MYSELF

LIST 3 THINGS YOU HAVE ALWAYS WANTED TO DO

LIFE IS GOOD BECAUSE...

_____

_____

_____

TODAY I FELT

SOMETHING GREAT THAT HAPPENED TODAY

_____

_____

_____

THIS PERSON BROUGHT ME JOY TODAY

_____

_____

DATE: S M T W TH F S ___/___/___

ONLY POSITIVE THOUGHTS IN MY DAY
I can make today awesome by:

_____

_____

_____

DRAW IT!
what are you looking forward to most today?

I LOVE MYSELF
LIST 3 THINGS YOU DREAM ABOUT

_ _ _ _ _ _ IS MY HERO BECAUSE.....

_____

_____

_____

TODAY I FELT

SOMETHING GREAT THAT HAPPENED TODAY

_____

_____

_____

THIS PERSON BROUGHT ME JOY TODAY

_____

_____

DATE: S M T W TH F S ___/___/___

ONLY POSITIVE THOUGHTS IN MY DAY
I can make today awesome by:

_____

_____

_____

DRAW IT!
what are you looking forward to most today?

I LOVE MYSELF
LIST 3 THINGS YOU HOPE TO DO THIS WEEK

TODAY I SMILED BECAUSE

_____

_____

_____

TODAY I FELT

SOMETHING GREAT THAT HAPPENED TODAY

_____

_____

_____

THIS PERSON BROUGHT ME JOY TODAY

_____

_____

DATE: S M T W TH F S ___/___/___

ONLY POSITIVE THOUGHTS IN MY DAY

I can make today awesome by:

_____

_____

_____

DRAW IT!

what are you looking forward to most today?

I LOVE MYSELF

LIST 3 THINGS YOU LOOK FORWARD TO

WHEN I FEEL MAD THIS IS WHAT I DO

_____

_____

_____

TODAY I FELT

SOMETHING GREAT THAT HAPPENED TODAY

_____

_____

_____

 THIS PERSON BROUGHT ME JOY TODAY

_____

_____

DATE: S M T W TH F S ___/___/___

ONLY POSITIVE THOUGHTS IN MY DAY
I can make today awesome by:

_____

_____

_____

DRAW IT!

what are you looking forward to most today?

I LOVE MYSELF
LIST 3 THINGS YOU DID THAT YOU WERE PROUD OF DOING

I'M GRATEFUL FOR

_____

_____

_____

TODAY I FELT

SOMETHING GREAT THAT HAPPENED TODAY

_____

_____

_____

THIS PERSON BROUGHT ME JOY TODAY

_____

_____

DATE: S M T W TH F S ___/___/___

ONLY POSITIVE THOUGHTS IN MY DAY
I can make today awesome by:

_____

_____

_____

DRAW IT!

what are you looking forward to most today?

I LOVE MYSELF
LIST 3 THINGS YOU ARE EXCITED ABOUT

WHAT I'M LOVING ABOUT LIFE RIGHT NOW

_____

_____

_____

TODAY I FELT

SOMETHING GREAT THAT HAPPENED TODAY

_____

_____

_____

 THIS PERSON BROUGHT ME JOY TODAY

_____

_____

DATE: S M T W TH F S   ___/___/___

ONLY POSITIVE THOUGHTS IN MY DAY
I can make today awesome by:

_____

_____

_____

DRAW IT!
what are you looking forward to most today?

I LOVE MYSELF
LIST 3 THINGS YOU ARE THANKFUL FOR

MY FAVORITE PERSON TO BE AROUND IS

_____

_____

_____

TODAY I FELT

SOMETHING GREAT THAT HAPPENED TODAY

_____

_____

_____

THIS PERSON BROUGHT ME JOY TODAY

_____

_____

DATE: S M T W TH F S ____/____/____

ONLY POSITIVE THOUGHTS IN MY DAY

I can make today awesome by:

_____

_____

_____

DRAW IT!

what are you looking forward to most today?

I LOVE MYSELF

LIST 3 WAYS YOUR LIFE IS AWESOME

THE PERSON I MOST ADMIRE IS

_____

_____

_____

TODAY I FELT

SOMETHING GREAT THAT HAPPENED TODAY

_____

_____

_____

THIS PERSON BROUGHT ME JOY TODAY

_____

_____

DATE: S M T W TH F S ___/___/___

ONLY POSITIVE THOUGHTS IN MY DAY
I can make today awesome by:

_____
_____
_____

DRAW IT!

what are you looking forward to most today?

I LOVE MYSELF
LIST 3 THINGS YOU DID THIS WEEK

THIS IS WHAT BRINGS ME HAPPINESS

_____

_____

_____

TODAY I FELT

SOMETHING GREAT THAT HAPPENED TODAY

_____

_____

_____

THIS PERSON BROUGHT ME JOY TODAY

_____

_____

DATE: S M T W TH F S ___/___/___

ONLY POSITIVE THOUGHTS IN MY DAY

I can make today awesome by:

_____

_____

_____

DRAW IT!

what are you looking forward to most today?

I LOVE MYSELF

LIST 3 SMALL SUCCESS YOU HAD THIS WEEK

THIS ALWAYS MAKES ME SMILE

_____

_____

_____

TODAY I FELT

SOMETHING GREAT THAT HAPPENED TODAY

_____

_____

_____

 THIS PERSON BROUGHT ME JOY TODAY

_____

_____

DATE: S M T W TH F S   ___/___/___

ONLY POSITIVE THOUGHTS IN MY DAY

I can make today awesome by:

_____

_____

_____

DRAW IT!

what are you looking forward to most today?

I LOVE MYSELF

LIST 3 THINGS YOU LIKE ABOUT YOURSELF

MY FAVORITE PART OF TODAY

_____

_____

_____

TODAY I FELT

SOMETHING GREAT THAT HAPPENED TODAY

_____

_____

_____

 THIS PERSON BROUGHT ME JOY TODAY

_____

_____

DATE: S M T W TH F S ___/___/___

ONLY POSITIVE THOUGHTS IN MY DAY
I can make today awesome by:

_____

_____

_____

DRAW IT!

what are you
looking forward
to most today?

I LOVE MYSELF
LIST 3 WORDS THAT DESCRIBE YOU

WHAT I'M LOOKING FORWARD TO TOMORROW

_____

_____

_____

TODAY I FELT

SOMETHING GREAT THAT HAPPENED TODAY

_____

_____

_____

THIS PERSON BROUGHT ME JOY TODAY

_____

_____

Made in the USA
Las Vegas, NV
18 August 2023